Gamma Hydra IV is swept by a mysterious radiation. And Kirk, Spock, McCoy and Scott are catapulted into a desperate race against time as they fight the rapid advance of aging, senility and death!

With command of the *Enterprise* torn from his grasp, Captain Kirk conceives a daring gamble to save the great starship and all on board from imminent annihilation...and halt the onslaught of...

THE DEADLY YEARS

OTHER **STAR TREK FOTONOVELS**™
you will enjoy—

STAR TREK ™*

THE DEADLY YEARS

Written by **DAVID P. HARMON**

adapted from the television series
created by **GENE RODDENBERRY**

BANTAM BOOKS
TORONTO · NEW YORK · LONDON

RLI: $\dfrac{\text{VLM 6 (VLR 5–7)}}{\text{IL 5}+}$

THE DEADLY YEARS

A Bantam Book / September 1978

Art Direction
Michael Parish, Los Angeles

Star Trek™ designates a trademark of
Paramount Pictures Corporation.

Fotonovel™ designates a trademark of
Mandala Productions.

ISBN 0-553-12028-X

Published simultaneously in the United States and Canada

PRINTED IN THE UNITED STATES OF AMERICA

0 9 8 7 6 5 4 3 2 1

Dear Readers:

We asked you to write us about your feelings a while ago, and the response has been overwhelming. We are glad to report that your approval has been greatly appreciated and your suggestions have been seriously considered. There is another interesting detail that we have noticed: every single reader names a few episodes as favorites. Our question: Why not name your six favorite episodes in order of preference and help Bantam Books and us in the selection of future books? At the same time we can have our "Star Trek all time favorites contest." Also please, include as always, any constructive suggestions that you may have.

MANDALA PRODUCTIONS
8831 Sunset Blvd.
Penthouse West
Los Angeles, CA 90069

Best regards,
MANDALA PRODUCTIONS

Dear Sirs:

I am a German S.T. fan and I was very pleased when I heard about your Fotonovels. In Germany, Fotonovels were published two years ago, but the quality was very bad and were published one page at a time in a magazine. Yours is one hundred times better. Could you publish a Star Trek Fotonovel every two weeks? I can't wait one whole month.

Matthias Terörde
Schonenberg 10
4290 Bocholt Germany

Dear Mandala:

I saw your S.T. Fotonovels on a shelf in a bookstore. I wanted to buy one but I had no money. So one day I asked my mother to get me one. Guess what happened the next day? I liked it so much I'm sending away for the rest.

Jurgen Reissing
New Market, Ontario
(8 years old)

CAST LIST

James T. Kirk, Captain
William Shatner

A man whose independent nature and compassionate heart make him a natural leader. His overriding concern is always the well-being of his ship and its crew which earns him their undying respect and love.

Spock, First Officer
Leonard Nimoy

Of Vulcan and Terran heritage, which accounts for his analytical mind and extraordinary strength. Logic and reason rule his life.

Leonard McCoy, M.D., Lt. Commander
DeForest Kelley

Senior Ship's Surgeon, head of Life Sciences Department. Though surrounded by the most advanced equipment the 24th Century can offer, he still practices more with his heart than his head.

Montgomery Scott, Lt. Commander
James Doohan

Chief Engineer. Unchallenged in his knowledge of the ship's engineering equipment. A veritable magician when it comes to seemingly impossible repairs.

Commodore George Stocker
Charles Drake

Dr. Janet Wallace
Sarah Marshall

**Lieutenant
Arlene Galway**
Beverly
Washburn

Pavel Chekov,
Ensign
Walter Koenig

Uhura
Lt. Communi-
cations Officer
Nichelle
Nichols

Sulu, Chief
Helmsman
George Takei

THE DEADLY YEARS

SPACE:

THE FINAL FRONTIER

THESE ARE THE VOYAGES OF THE STARSHIP "ENTERPRISE." ITS FIVE-YEAR MISSION: TO EXPLORE STRANGE NEW WORLDS, TO SEEK OUT NEW LIFE, NEW CIVILIZATIONS, TO BOLDLY GO WHERE NO MAN HAS GONE BEFORE.

EN ROUTE TO STARBASE 10, WHERE
OUR PASSENGER, COMMODORE
STOCKER, WILL ASSUME COMMAND
OF STARBASE OPERATIONS, WE ARE
STOPPING AT GAMMA HYDRA IV TO
DELIVER SUPPLIES AND MAKE THE
ROUTINE ANNUAL CHECK OF THE
SCIENCE COLONY THERE.

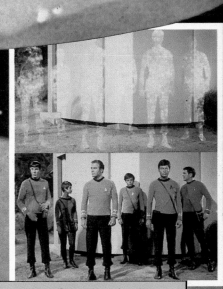

From the orbiting Starship, a landing party beams to the surface of the planet...to materialize fully as the transporter's matter-to-energy-to-matter process is completed.

Scanning his tricorder, Chekov enters the darkened building...

...and straining to see in the gloom, touches something just as the room is suddenly bathed in light.

Cold and rigid, a corpse lies before him, its visage ravaged by time...a stark biography etched in dead flesh.

As if he had touched a branding iron, Chekov snatches his hand away from the stiff arm...and a strangled cry lodges in his throat.

Despising his panic, he runs, screaming, from the building...unable to disguise the fear in his voice.

Captain! Captain!

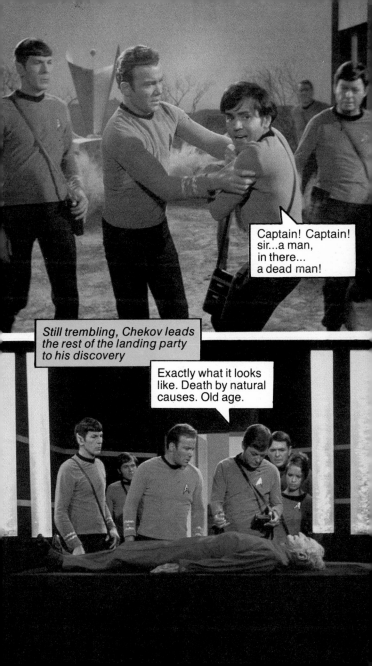

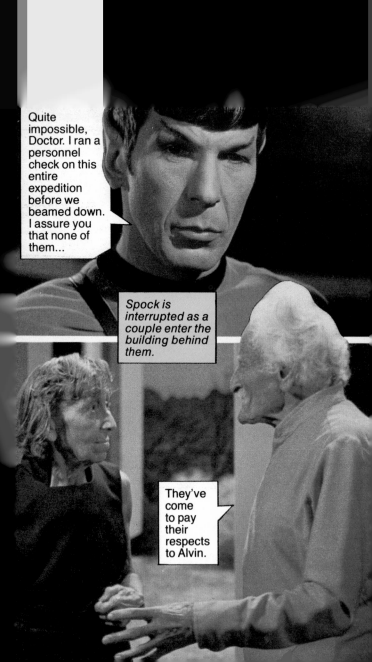

CAPTAINS LOG:

STARDATE 3478.3

ON A ROUTINE MISSION TO RE-SUPPLY THE EXPERIMENTAL COLONY AT GAMMA HYDRA IV, WE DISCOVERED A MOST UNUSUAL PHENOMENON. OF THE SIX MEMBERS OF THE COLONY...NONE OF WHOM WERE OVER THIRTY...WE FOUND FOUR HAD DIED AND TWO WERE DYING OF OLD AGE. WE HAVE BEAMED THOSE TWO ABOARD UNDER DR. MCCOY'S SUPERVISION.

In Sickbay aboard the Enterprise the Biocomp readouts above the beds of Robert and Elaine Johnson provide a graphic display of fading life-signs.

Mister Johnson, can you hear me?

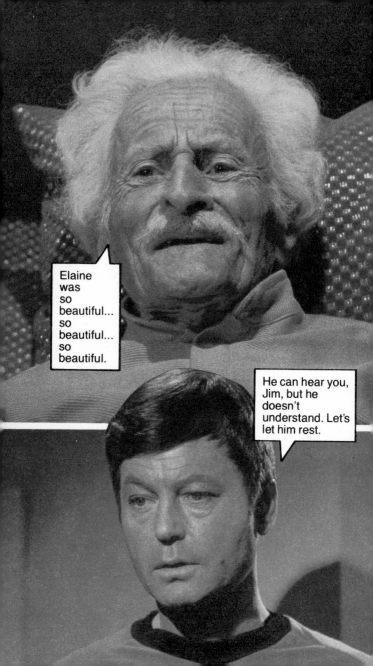

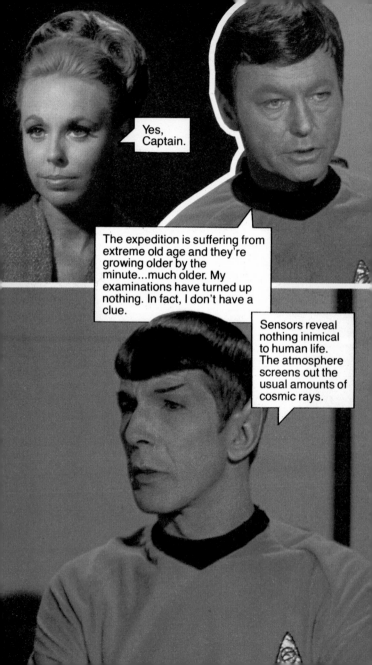

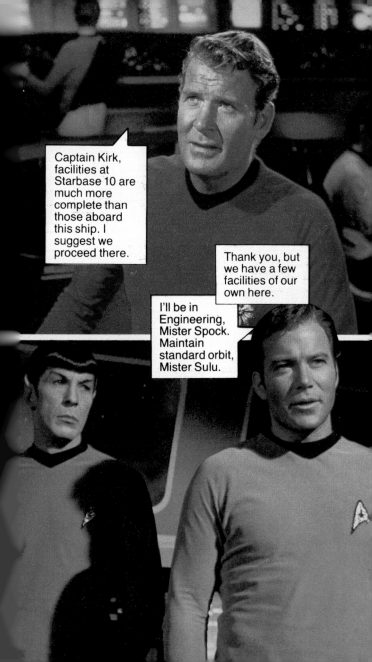

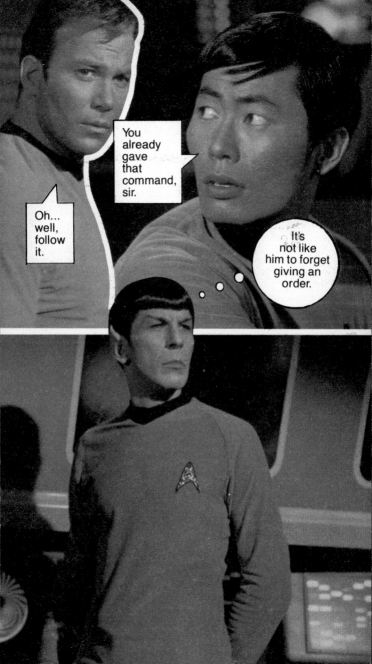

Turning at a sound in the doorway, Kirk and McCoy are aghast at the sight of Engineer Scott, looking twenty years older.

Scotty!

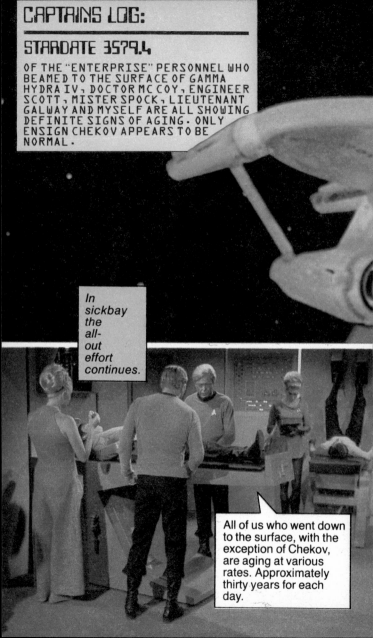

CAPTAINS LOG:

STARDATE 3579.4

OF THE "ENTERPRISE" PERSONNEL WHO BEAMED TO THE SURFACE OF GAMMA HYDRA IV, DOCTOR MC COY, ENGINEER SCOTT, MISTER SPOCK, LIEUTENANT GALWAY AND MYSELF ARE ALL SHOWING DEFINITE SIGNS OF AGING. ONLY ENSIGN CHEKOV APPEARS TO BE NORMAL.

In sickbay the all-out effort continues.

All of us who went down to the surface, with the exception of Chekov, are aging at various rates. Approximately thirty years for each day.

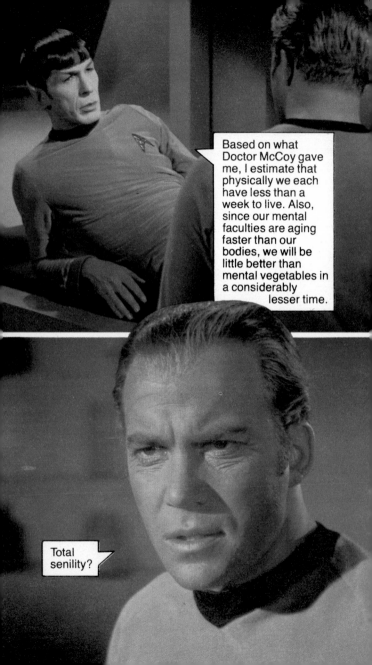

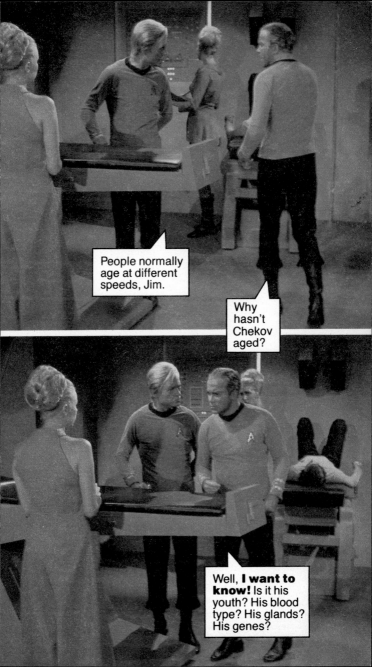

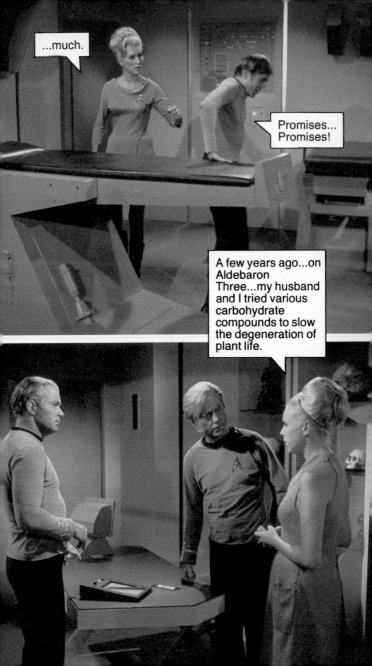

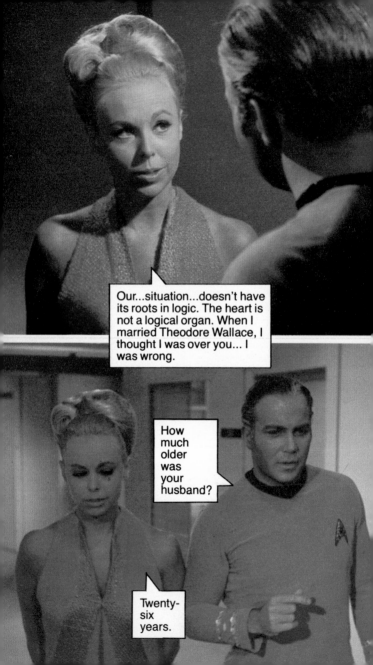

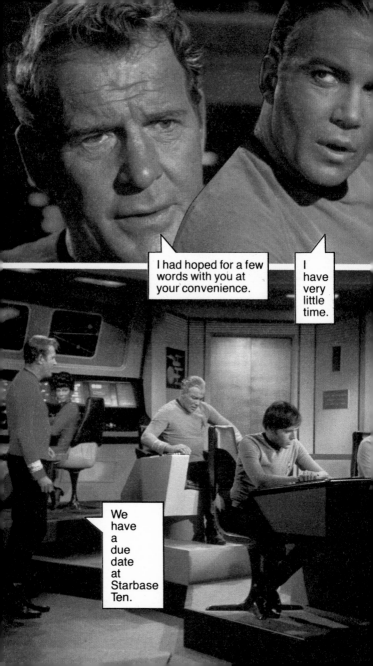

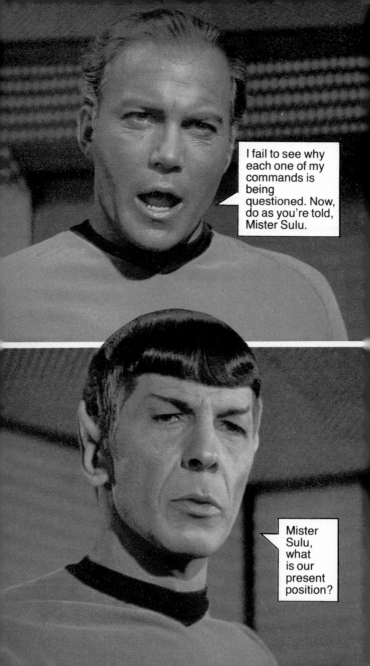

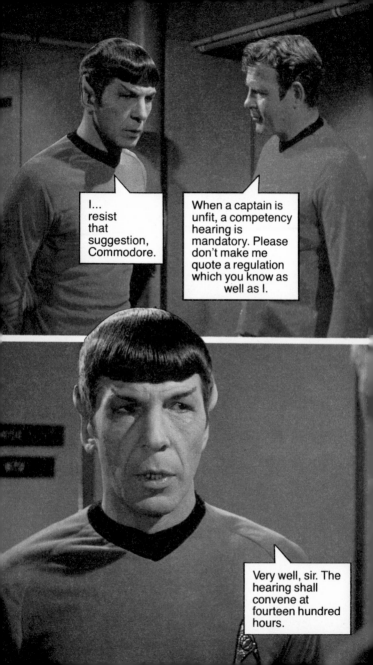

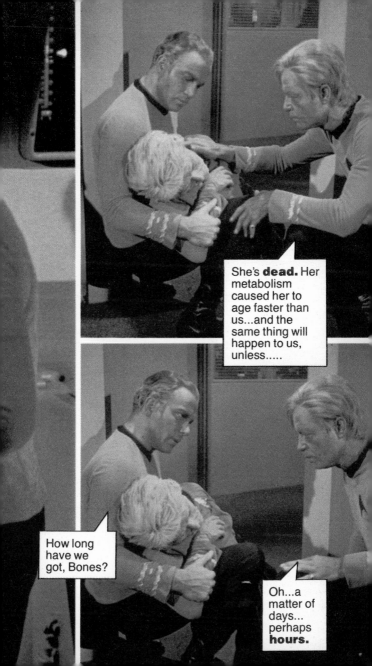

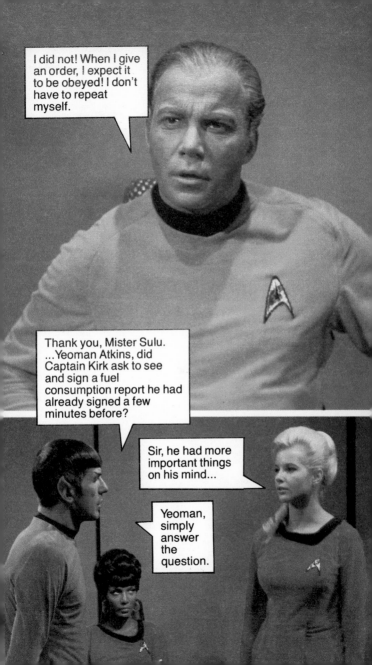

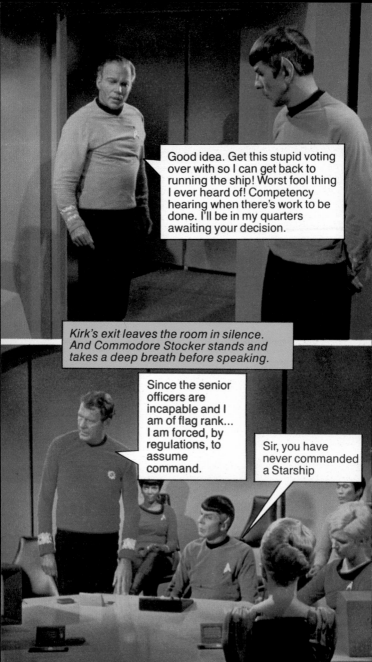

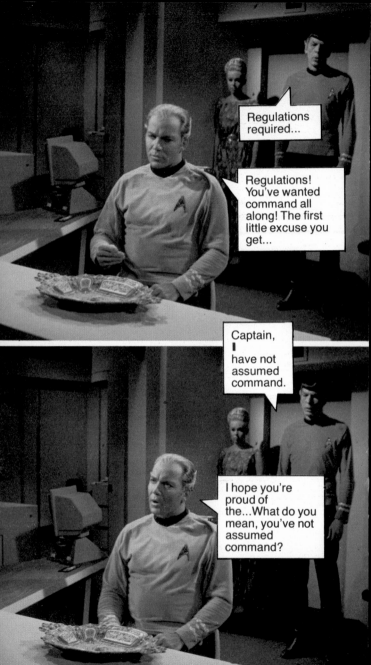

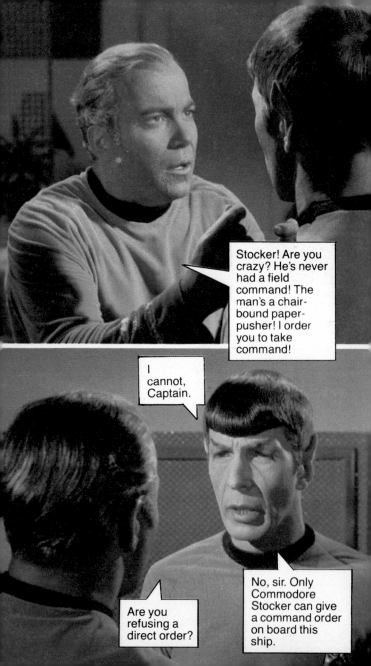

Kirk leaves his quarters and, out of habit, heads for the bridge. Then, feeling unwanted and suddenly outraged, he takes a turbo-lift to the seventh deck, to check on McCoy's progress in Sickbay.

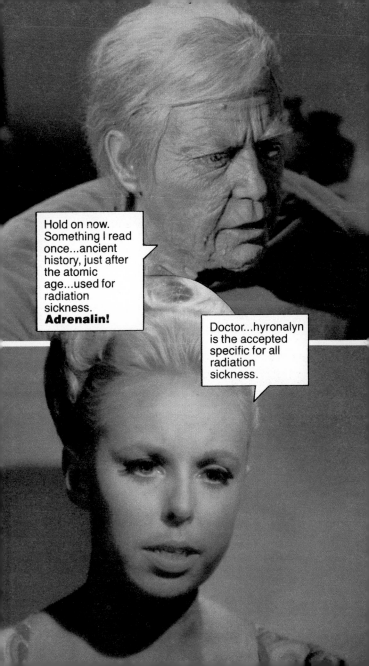

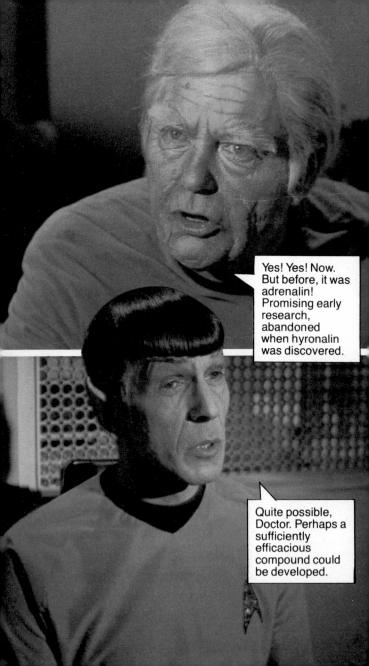

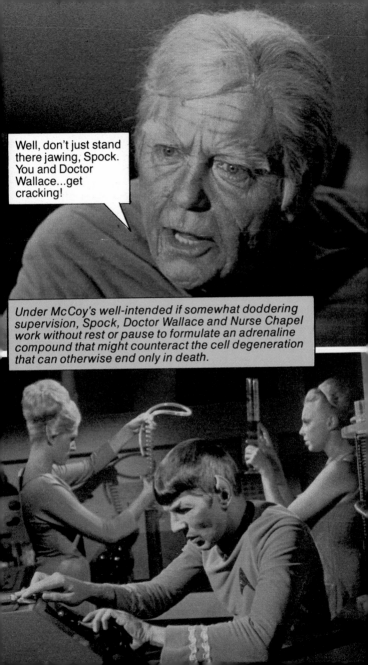

Stocker's mind races through an array of command possibilities. And he stares, frozen with indecision, at the main screen... at the highly magnified image of a Romulan "Bird of Prey" war-ship, closing at hyper-light speed.

From Romulan ships still hundreds of thousands of kilometers distant, photon torpedos track and converge upon the Enterprise. And the great ship trembles as her defectors ward off a terrible pounding.

The pounding of the Enterprise continues and on the bridge, Stocker arrives at a decision.

They won't listen, sir. We've tangled with them before.

Try to raise the Romulans. If we could talk to them...explain why we've violated the neutral zone...

The photon torpedos, a Romulan invention, keep coming. And the screen fills with the glare of the huge "fire-balls" as the ship's deflectors, already weakening, buffer the force of the explosions.

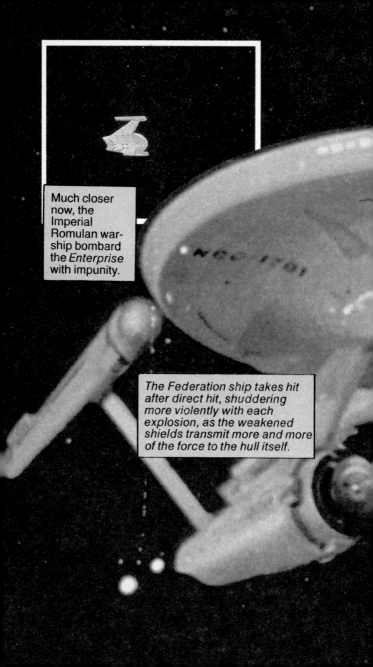

Much closer now, the Imperial Romulan warship bombard the *Enterprise* with impunity.

The Federation ship takes hit after direct hit, shuddering more violently with each explosion, as the weakened shields transmit more and more of the force to the hull itself.

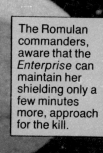

The Romulan commanders, aware that the *Enterprise* can maintain her shielding only a few minutes more, approach for the kill.

In Sickbay, aboard the Enterprise, *McCoy's impaired vision prevents him from witnessing the effect of the serum on Kirk.*

Well...well, what's happening?

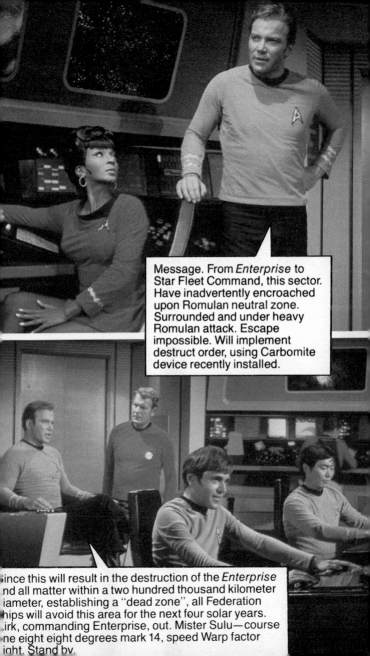

That is very considerate of you, Doctor.

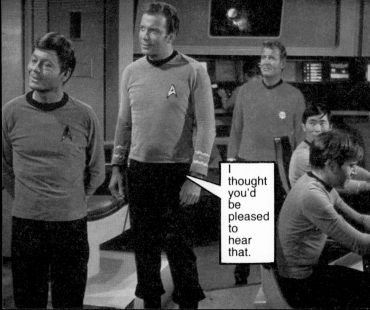

I thought you'd be pleased to hear that.

GLOSSARY

Adrenaline—An endocrine fluid produced in the ectodermal medulla of the adrenal gland in mammals. A regulator of metabolic function.

Comet—A celestial body consisting of a fuzzy head usually surrounding a bright nucleus, with an orbit varying in eccentricity between nearly circular and parabolic.

Corbomite device—A nonexistent invention ostensibly capable of immense destruction, used more than once by Captain Kirk as a successful bluff.

Commodore—In Star Fleet terms, an officer of flag rank, above a Fleet Captain and below an Admiral.

Competency Hearing—A preliminary examination of an officer's professional capabilities, usually convened only in extreme circumstances by another officer of command rank.

Hyronalin—A specific for radiation poisoning superceding adrenaline after the radiation wars.

Medical Computer—A diagnostic tool capable of gathering, interpreting and evaluating biological data relating to the physical condition of a number of species.

Romulan Empire—A military dictatorship extending over a large sector of the galaxy, peopled by a race biologically similar to the Vulcans, but without the Vulcan reverence for logic. The Romulans sustain a rather hostile truce with the United Federation of Planets.

Romulan neutral zone—An area between Romulan and Federation territory, entry into which by either party can be considered an act of war.

Starbase—Federation-maintained bases in space, with facilities for docking, repair, supply, shore leave, etc.

STAR TREK QUIZ #11

In each question below, circle the one answer that best completes this sentence.

1. On Gamma Hydra IV, Ensign Chekov was frightened by:
   a. a deadly virus
   b. the sight of a corpse
   c. a surge of adrenaline
   d. a surge of hyronalin

2. Commodore Stocker was impatient to assume command of:
   a. the Starship *Enterprise*
   b. Gamma Hydra IV
   c. Starbase Ten
   d. Star Fleet

3. The third person to die on board the Enterprise as a result of the Gamma Hydra IV radiation was:
   a. Robert Johnson
   b. Lieutenant Galway
   c. Doctor Janet Wallace
   d. Chief Engineer Scott

4. Kirk, Spock, McCoy and Scott were deteriorating faster mentally than they were physically.
   a. True
   b. False

5. Commodore Stocker asked Mr. Spock to convene a hearing to determine Captain Kirk's:
   a. true physical age
   b. loyalty
   c. professional capability
   d. attitude

6. Doctor McCoy agreed with the medical computer's evaluation of Captain Kirk's physical age.

   a. True
   b. False

7. Mr. Spock aged less rapidly than Kirk, Scott, or McCoy because of his:

   a. longer life-span
   b. disciplined mind
   c. greater height
   d. natural stubbornness

8. Surrounded by Romulan battle-cruisers, Commodore Stocker was able to make command decisions easily.

   a. True
   b. False

9. The first draught of hydroxalene serum was drunk by:

   a. Mister Spock
   b. Captain Kirk
   c. Doctor McCoy
   d. Ensign Chekov

10. The Corbomite device is:

   a. a Romulan invention
   b. fictitious
   c. a secret Federation weapon
   d. a product of Klingon technology

Turn the page for the answers.

Spock. Half Vulcan, half human. And something in his green Vulcan blood is driving him, compelling him, to return to Vulcan, to mate...or **die!!**

Thus, Captain Kirk, Mister Spock and Doctor McCoy are thrust into one of their strangest adventures yet, in which the three stand together in a mystery-shrouded ceremony as ancient as Vulcan culture. A brutal rite which, for one of them, must end in **death!**

Kirk weighs a friendship against his command, his career...and his life before he can understand the meaning of...

AMOK TIME

DON'T MISS THIS ONE! COMING SOON, WHEREVER PAPERBACKS ARE SOLD

ANSWERS to Quiz on preceeding pages:
1. **b** 2. **c** 3. **b** 4. **a** 5. **c**
6. **a** 7. **a** 8. **b** 9. **b** 10. **b**